7x¹¹/₁₃ ≈ 9/13

DINOSAUR PROFILES

STEGOSAURUS

Titles in the Dinosaur Profiles series include:

DINOSAUR PROFILES

STEGOSAURUS

Text by Fabio Marco Dalla Vecchia
Illustrations by Leonello Calvetti and Luca Massini

BLACKBIRCH®
PRESS

THOMSON
★
GALE

San Diego • Detroit • New York • San Francisco • Cleveland • New Haven, Conn. • Waterville, Maine • London • Munich

For more information, contact
The Gale Group, Inc.
27500 Drake Rd.
Farmington Hills, MI 48331-3535
Or you can visit our Internet site at http://www.gale.com

Computer illustrations 3D and 2D: Leonello Calvetti and Luca Massini

Photographs: pages 22, 23 François Gohier/Ardea London

LIBRARY OF CONGRESS CATALOGING-IN-PUBLICATION DATA

Dalla Vecchia, Fabio Marco.
 Stegosaurus / text by Fabio Marco Dalla Vecchia; illustrations by Leonello Calvetti and Luca Massini.
  p. cm. — (Dinosaur profiles)
 Includes bibliographical references and index.
 ISBN 1-4103-0495-7 (paperback : alk. paper)
 ISBN 1-4103-0330-6 (hardback : alk. paper)
 1. Stegosaurus—Juvenile literature. I. Calvetti, Leonello. II. Massini, Luca. III. Title. IV. Series: Dalla Vecchia, Fabio Marco. Dinosaur profiles.
 QE862.O65D37 2004
 567.915′3—dc22   2004008699

Contents

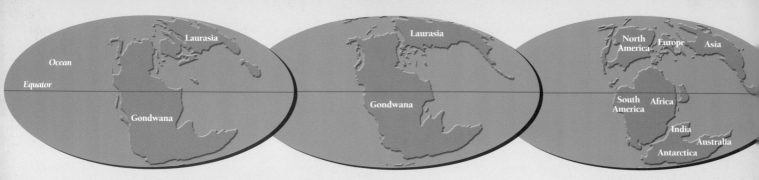

Late Triassic
227–206 million years ago

Early Jurassic
206–176 million years ago

Middle Jurassic
176–159 million years ago

A Changing World

Earth's long history began 4.6 billion years ago. Dinosaurs are some of the most fascinating animals from the planet's long past.

The word *dinosaur* comes from the word *dinosauria*. This word was invented by the English scientist Richard Owen in 1842. It comes from two Greek words, *deinos* and *sauros*. Together, these words mean "terrifying lizards."

The dinosaur era, also called the Mesozoic era, lasted from 248 million years ago to 65 million years ago. It is divided into three periods. The first, the Triassic period, lasted 42 million years. The second, the Jurassic period, lasted 61 million years. The third, the Cretaceous period, lasted 79 million years. Dinosaurs ruled the world for a huge time span of 160 million years.

Like dinosaurs, mammals appeared at the end of the Triassic period. During the time of dinosaurs, mammals were small animals the size of a mouse. Only after dinosaurs became extinct did mammals develop into the many forms that exist today. Humans never met Mesozoic dinosaurs. The dinosaurs were gone nearly 65 million years before humans appeared on Earth.

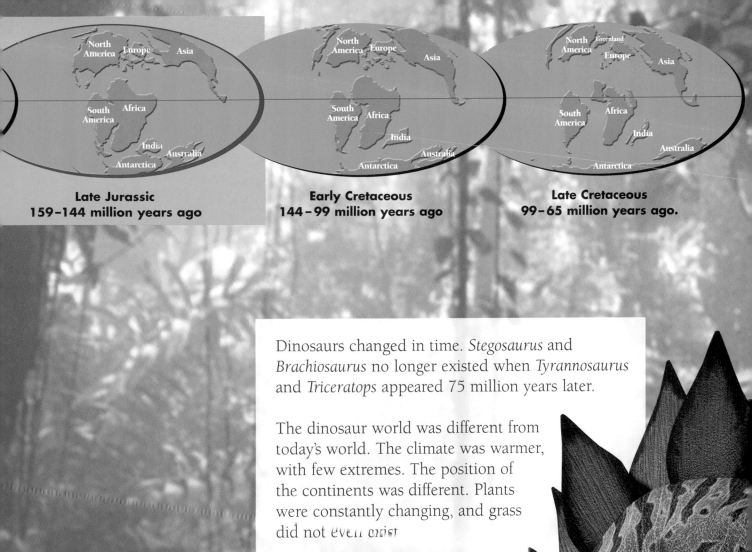

Late Jurassic
159–144 million years ago

Early Cretaceous
144–99 million years ago

Late Cretaceous
99–65 million years ago.

Dinosaurs changed in time. *Stegosaurus* and *Brachiosaurus* no longer existed when *Tyrannosaurus* and *Triceratops* appeared 75 million years later.

The dinosaur world was different from today's world. The climate was warmer, with few extremes. The position of the continents was different. Plants were constantly changing, and grass did not even exist

An Armored Giant

Stegosaurus was an ornithischian dinosaur belonging to the group *Stegosauria*, or stegosaurians. They are best known for the large plates on their backs. The plates were in two rows. A plate in one row would be opposite the empty space between two plates in the other row.

Scientists have different ideas about the purpose of these plates. At first, it was thought that they were used only for defense. Then it was discovered that they were supplied with blood. This led scientists to believe that the plates helped control a stegosaur's body temperature. When its body temperature became too high, blood was pumped into the plates. The blood in the plates cooled down before returning to the body. This helped lower the dinosaur's body temperature. Another possible use for the plates was as a display to attract females or to warn off predators.

Stegosaurus had other unusual features. Its throat and the underside of its neck were protected by smaller, semi-circular bony plates. It also had long spikes at the end of its tail.

An adult *Stegosaurus* was 17 to 24 feet (5 to 7 m) long. It weighed about 2.4 to 4.4 tons (2.2 to 4 metric tons). Its front legs were much shorter than its back legs. It probably moved only on all four limbs. Some paleontologists believe it could stand up on its back legs to reach the highest parts of trees, however. It was probably very slow and clumsy.

Stegosaurus lived in North America at the end of the Late Jurassic period 155 to 148 million years ago. Fossils have been found in Colorado, Utah, Wyoming, and New Mexico. At the end of the Jurassic period, there were stegosaurians living in Europe, Africa, Asia, and North America. By the beginning of the Cretaceous, however, they were already very rare. They died out before the end of the Cretaceous period.

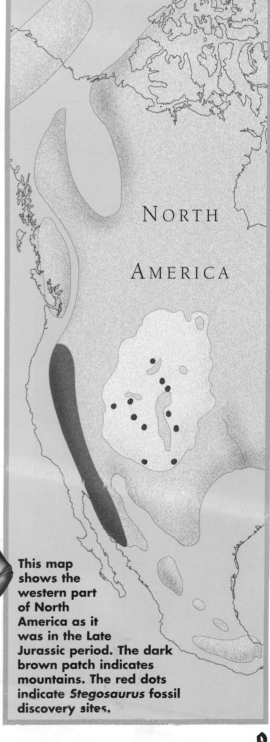

NORTH

AMERICA

This map shows the western part of North America as it was in the Late Jurassic period. The dark brown patch indicates mountains. The red dots indicate *Stegosaurus* fossil discovery sites.

THIRST

One problem that the stegosaurs faced again and again was drought. When the dry season lasted longer than usual, watering holes dried up, leaving muddy pools. Herds of dinosaurs crowded around these pools looking for a sip of water. Many weak and tired animals ended up stuck in the mud and starved to death. Predators tried to take advantage of these trapped animals, but they sometimes ended up victims of the quicksand themselves.

DEFENSE

Stegosaurus was a slow animal. It could not make a fast escape from a predator. Instead, it had to defend itself. The large plates on its back, tail, and neck made it hard for predators to bite those parts of its body. A predator could not bite the end of its tail, either, because of the four long spikes there. The spikes could also be used as weapons if the *Stegosaurus* swung its tail at an attacker. Despite these tools, *Allosaurus*, the most common flesh-eating dinosaur in North America at that time, probably tried to kill and eat stegosaurs.

THE STEGOSAURUS BODY

Despite its large size, *Stegosaurus* had a small head and a very small brain. It had one of the smallest brains of all the large dinosaurs. It was the size of a walnut and weighed only 2.5 ounces (70 g). An African elephant is about the same size as a stegosaur, but its brain weighs fifty times more. Although the brain was small, the parts of it that control smell and sight were very well developed. *Stegosaurus*'s strong sense of sight and smell helped it identify predators before they attacked.

A *Stegosaurus*'s teeth were very different from those of most other dinosaurs. They were small and leaf shaped.

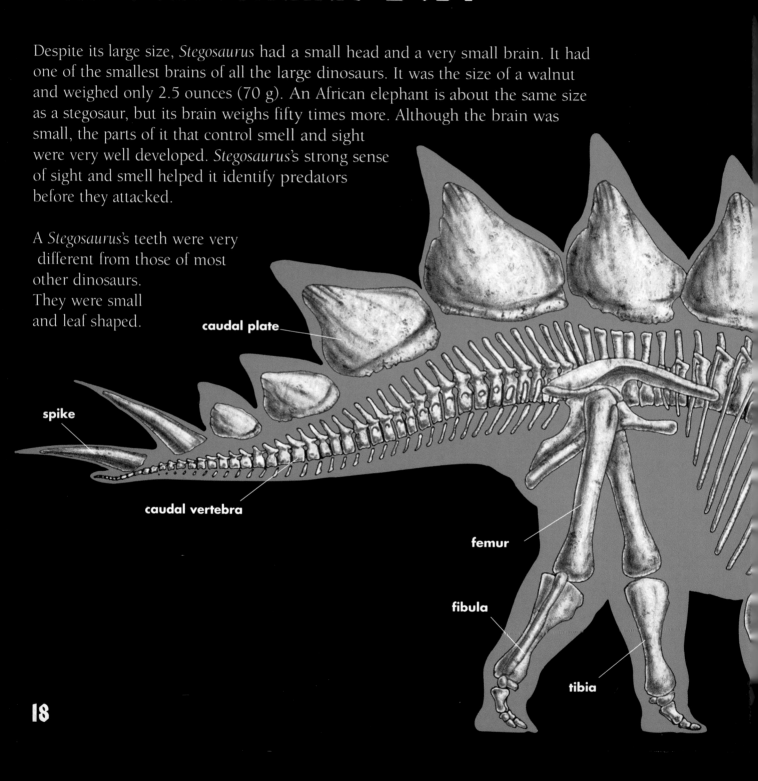

caudal plate

spike

caudal vertebra

femur

fibula

tibia

Today, they are very easy to identify even if the fossil is incomplete.

The plates on its back were 2 feet (60 cm) tall. The spines at the end of the tail could reach 40 inches (1 m) in length.

Stegosaurus's back feet each had three toes with small hooves. The smaller front feet left a footprint with five toe prints, one of which was very small. Few *Stegosaurus* footprints have been found.

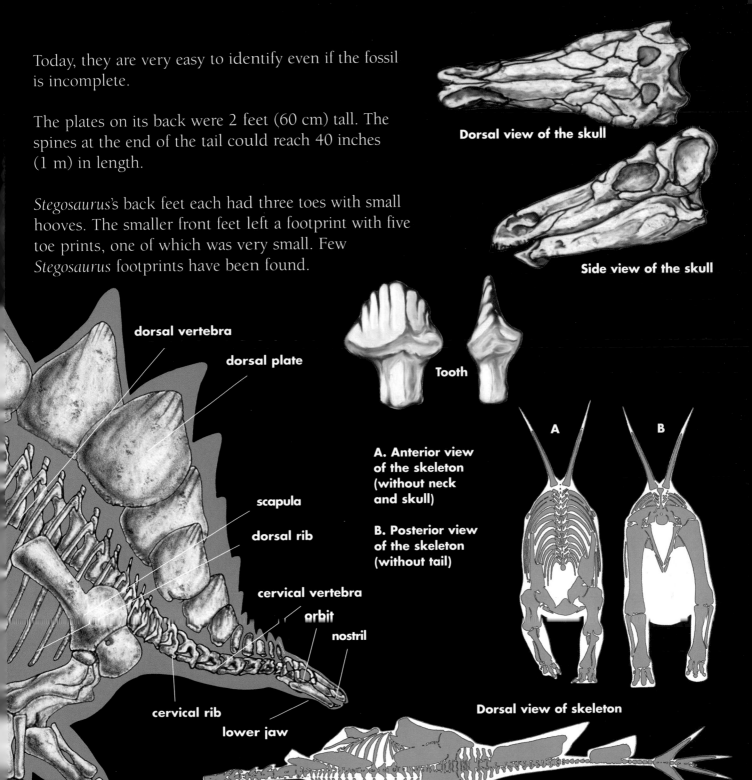

Dorsal view of the skull

Side view of the skull

dorsal vertebra

dorsal plate

Tooth

scapula

dorsal rib

A. Anterior view of the skeleton (without neck and skull)

B. Posterior view of the skeleton (without tail)

cervical vertebra

orbit

nostril

A

B

cervical rib

lower jaw

Dorsal view of skeleton

19

Digging Up Stegosaurus

The first *Stegosaurus* skeleton was found in Colorado in 1877. Paleontologist Othniel C. Marsh named it after the Greek words for "roofed reptile" because of the plates on its back. He thought the plates laid flat on the animal's back, like tiles on a roof.

Stegosaurus fossils are rare. Most of them were collected between 1877 and 1887 in Colorado and Wyoming. The most complete skeleton discovered in that period, and also the most famous, was found near Cañon City, Colorado. It was collected by M.P. Felch in 1885. This fossil is known as "road kill" because of how it was preserved. The rock looks like it was crushed by a car. The carcass of the animal was probably carried in a stream for only a short distance before it was covered by sediment. The skeleton is very complete. The large plates on the back are in their natural upright position. In the early 1990s, a nearly complete skeleton was found by paleontologist Bryan Small near the place "road kill" was discovered.

The "road kill" specimen is on display at the National Museum of Natural History in Washington, D.C. The skeleton found by Bryan Small is at the Denver Museum of Nature and Science in Colorado. Other skeletons can be seen at the Carnegie Museum of Pittsburgh and at the American Museum of Natural History in New York.

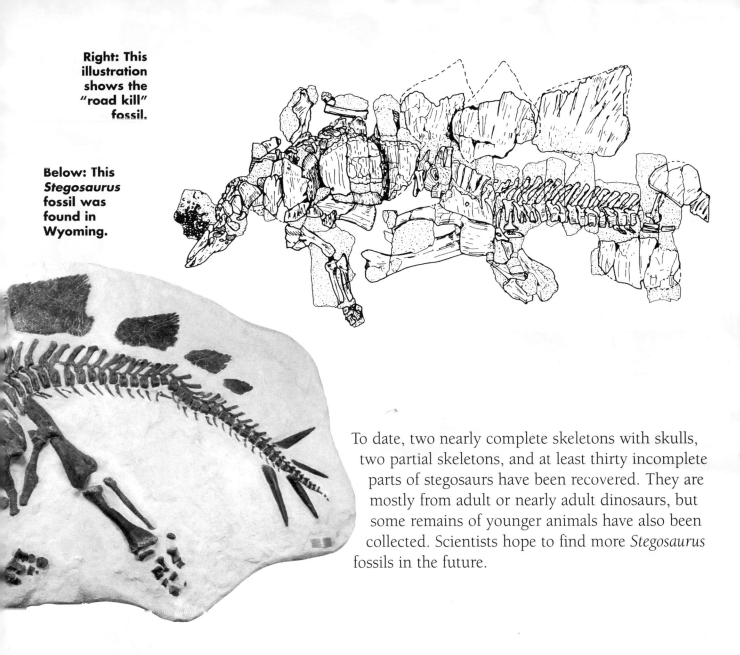

Right: This illustration shows the "road kill" fossil.

Below: This *Stegosaurus* fossil was found in Wyoming.

To date, two nearly complete skeletons with skulls, two partial skeletons, and at least thirty incomplete parts of stegosaurs have been recovered. They are mostly from adult or nearly adult dinosaurs, but some remains of younger animals have also been collected. Scientists hope to find more *Stegosaurus* fossils in the future.

Places where stegosaurian fossils have been found are noted on the map.

Many scientists believe that the Chicxulub crater off the coast of Mexico was made by a meteorite that led to the extinction of the dinosaurs.

At least three different species of *Stegosaurus* are known: *Stegosaurus stenops*, *Stegosaurus armatus*, and *Stegosaurus longispinus*. Its closest relatives were *Kentrosaurus* in Tanzania, Africa, and *Wuerhosaurus* in China. They differ mainly in the shape of their plates and spikes.

● *Wuerhosaurus*, China, 144–100 million years ago

● *Kentrosaurus*, Tanzania, 155–145 million years ago

STEGOSAURS

● *Stegosaurus,*
USA, 154–148
million years ago

Sixty-five million years ago, 80 million years after the time of *Stegosaurus*, dinosaurs became extinct. This may have happened because a large meteorite struck Earth. A wide crater caused by a meteorite exactly 65 million years ago has been located along the coast of the Yucatán Peninsula in Mexico. The impact of the meteorite would have produced an enormous amount of dust. This dust would have stayed suspended in the atmosphere and blocked sunlight for a long time. A lack of sunlight would have caused a drastic drop of the earth's temperature and killed plants. The plant-eating dinosaurs would have died, starved and frozen. As a result, meat-eating dinosaurs would have had no prey and would also have starved.

Some scientists believe dinosaurs did not die out completely. They think that birds were feathered dinosaurs that survived the great extinction. That would make the present-day chicken and all of its feathered relatives descendants of the large dinosaurs.

THE EVOLUTION OF DINOSAURS

The oldest dinosaur fossils are 220–225 million years old and have been found mainly in South America. They have also been found in Africa, India, and North America. Dinosaurs probably evolved from small and nimble bipedal reptiles like the Triassic *Lagosuchus* of Argentina. Dinosaurs were able to rule the world because their legs were held directly under the body, like those of modern mammals. This made them faster and less clumsy than other reptiles.

Since 1887, dinosaurs have been divided into two groups based on the structure of their hips. Saurischian dinosaurs had hips shaped like those of modern lizards. Ornithischian dinosaurs had hips shaped like those of modern birds.

Triceratops is one of the Ornithischian dinosaurs, whose hip bones (inset) are shaped like those of modern birds.

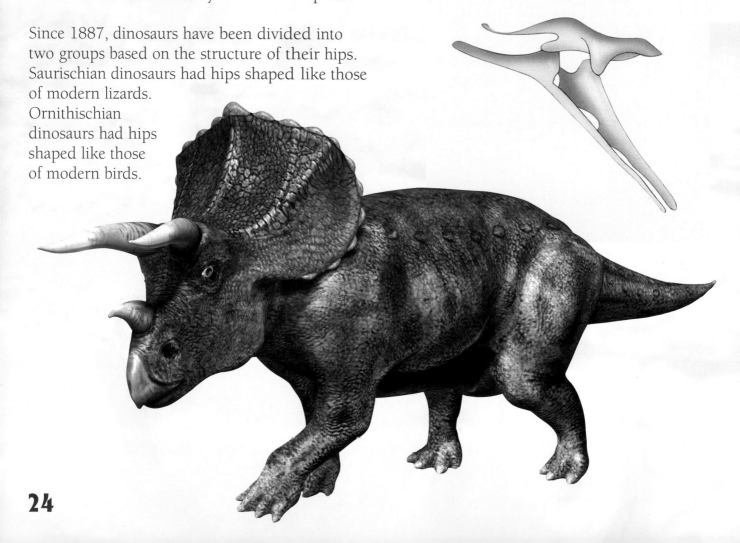

24

Tyrannosaurus is in the Saurischian group of dinosaurs, whose hip bones (inset) are shaped like those of modern lizards.

There are two main groups of saurischians. One group is sauropodomorphs. This group includes sauropods, such as *Brachiosaurus*. Sauropods ate plants and were quadrupedal, meaning they walked on four legs. The other group of saurischians, theropods, includes bipedal meat-eating predators. Some paleontologists believe birds are a branch of theropod dinosaurs.

Ornithischians are all plant eaters. They are divided into three groups. Thyreophorans include the quadrupedal stegosaurians, including *Stegosaurus*, and ankylosaurians, including *Ankylosaurus*. The other two groups are ornithopods, which includes *Edmontosaurus* and marginocephalians.

25

A DINOSAUR'S FAMILY TREE

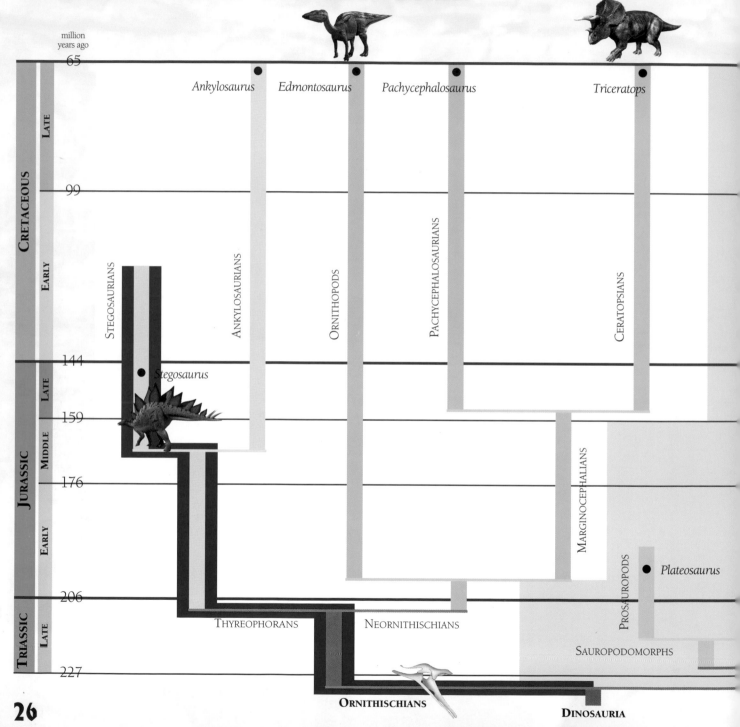

million
years ago

CRETACEOUS

LATE

EARLY

JURASSIC

LATE

MIDDLE

EARLY

TRIASSIC

LATE

65

99

144

159

176

206

227

Ankylosaurus

Edmontosaurus

Pachycephalosaurus

Triceratops

STEGOSAURIANS

ANKYLOSAURIANS

ORNITHOPODS

PACHYCEPHALOSAURIANS

CERATOPSIANS

Stegosaurus

MARGINOCEPHALIANS

PROSAUROPODS

Plateosaurus

THYREOPHORANS

NEORNITHISCHIANS

SAUROPODOMORPHS

ORNITHISCHIANS

DINOSAURIA

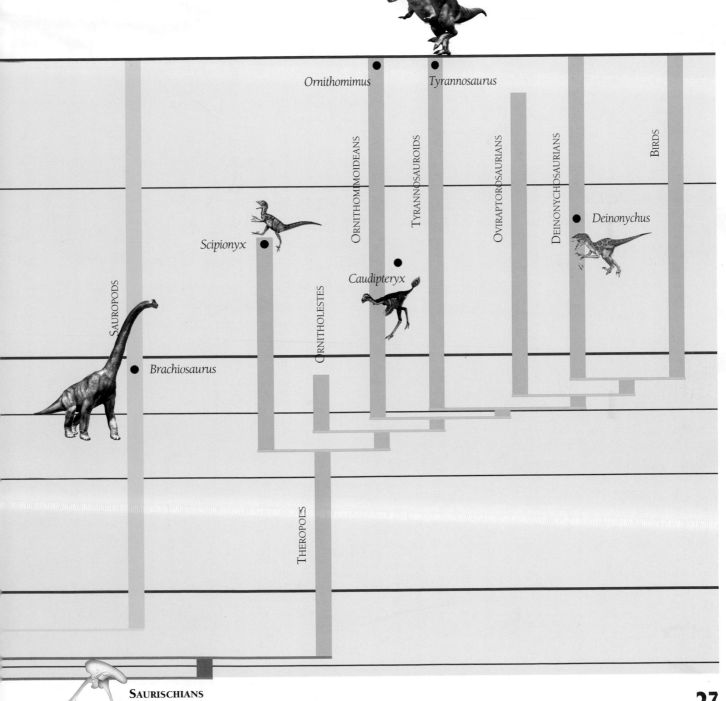

Ornithomimus

Tyrannosaurus

ORNITHOMIMOIDEANS

TYRANNOSAUROIDS

OVIRAPTOROSAURIANS

DEINONYCHOSAURIANS

BIRDS

Deinonychus

Scipionyx

Caudipteryx

SAUROPODS

ORNITHOLESTES

Brachiosaurus

THEROPODS

SAURISCHIANS

27

Glossary

Bipedal moving on two feet

Bone hard tissue made mainly of calcium phosphate

Caudal related to the tail

Cervical related to the neck

Cretaceous Period the period of geological time between 144 and 65 million years ago

Dorsal related to the back

Egg a large cell enclosed in a shell produced by reptiles and birds to reproduce themselves

Evolution changes in organisms over time

Feathers outgrowth of the skin of birds and some dinosaurs, used for flight

Femur thigh bone

Fibula the outer of the two bones in the lower leg

Fossil a part of an organism of an earlier geologic age, such as a skeleton or leaf imprint, that has been preserved in the earth's crust

Jurassic Period the period of geological time between 206 and 144 million years ago

Mesozoic Era the period of geological time between 248 and 65 million years ago

Meteorite a piece of iron or rock that falls to Earth from space

Orbit the opening in the skull surrounding the eye

Pack a group of predator animals hunting together

Paleontologist a scientist who studies prehistoric life

Quicksand loose sand mixed with water in which animals can get trapped and sink

Quadrupedal moving on four feet

Savanna a plain containing scattered trees

Scapula shoulder blade

Skeleton the structure of an animal body, made up of bones

Skull the bones that form the cranium and face

Tibia the shinbone

Triassic Period the period of geological time between 248 and 206 million years ago

Vertebrae the bones of the backbone

FOR MORE INFORMATION

Books

Paul M. Barrett, *National Geographic Dinosaurs*.
Washington, DC: National Geographic Society, 2001.

Tim Haines, *Walking with Dinosaurs: A Natural History*.
New York: Dorling Kindersley, 2000.

David Lambert, Darren Naish, and Elizabeth Wyse,
*Dinosaur Encyclopedia: From Dinosaurs to the Dawn of
Man*. New York: Dorling Kindersley, 2001.

Web Sites

The Cyberspace Museum of Natural History
www.cyberspacemuseum.com/dinohall.html
An online dinosaur museum that includes descriptions and illustrations.

Dinodata
www.dinodata.net
A site that includes detailed descriptions of fossils,
illustrations, and news about dinosaur research and
recent discoveries.

**The Smithsonian National Museum of Natural
History**
www.nmnh.si.edu/paleo/dino
A virtual tour of the Smithsonian's National Museum
of Natural History dinosaur exhibits.

About the Author

Fabio Marco Dalla Vecchia is the curator of the Paleontological Museum of Monfalcone in Gorizia, Italy. He has participated in several paleontological field works in Italy and other countries and has directed paleontological excavations in Italy. He is the author of more than fifty scientific articles that have been published in national and international journals.

INDEX

Index